BYSTANDER POWER

Now with Anti-Bullying Action!

by Phyllis Kaufman Goodstein
& Elizabeth Verdick

Illustrated by Steve Mark

free spirit
PUBLISHING®

Library of Congress Cataloging-in-Publication Data

Goodstein, Phyllis Kaufman.

Bystander power : now with anti-bullying action / Phyllis Kaufman Goodstein, Elizabeth Verdick.

p. cm. — (Laugh & learn)

"A book in the Laugh & Learn series."

Includes bibliographical references and index.

ISBN 978-1-57542-411-8 — ISBN 1-57542-411-8 1. Bullying—Juvenile literature. 2. Bullying—Prevention—Juvenile literature. 3. Bullying in schools—Prevention—Juvenile literature. I. Verdick, Elizabeth. II. Title.

BF637.B85G66 2012

302.34'3—dc23

2012010428

eBook ISBN: 978-1-57542-657-0

Reading Level Grade 4; Interest Level Ages 8–13;
Fountas & Pinnell Guided Reading Level R

Edited by Eric Braun
Cover design by Tasha Kenyon
Interior design by Michelle Lee

10 9 8 7 6 5 4 3 2 1
Printed in Hong Kong
P17200512

Free Spirit Publishing Inc.
Minneapolis, MN
(612) 338-2068
help4kids@freespirit.com
www.freespirit.com

FSC
www.fsc.org
MIX
Paper from
responsible sources
FSC® C018769

Free Spirit offers competitive pricing.
Contact edsales@freespirit.com for pricing information on
multiple quantity purchases.

Dedication

To Arnie, Eric, Steven, Ellen, George, Marc,
Debra, Eytan, Micah, Steven, Sam, Paul, Karen,
Danny, David, Brian, Gloria, and my mother
and father for being Upstanders in my life.
—PKG

To every kid who's ever been bullied and to all
you bystanders who want to make changes:
you're not alone, stay strong!
—EV

Acknowledgments

Ellen Bennet, Linda Greenzang, Maryrose Krassner, and Martha Posso read the original manuscript and offered recommendations. Naomi Drew, M.A., also gave suggestions. The intelligent, thoughtful, and thorough responses Jessica Goldberg and Katlin Mary O'Neill gave to educational questions were invaluable. Thank you all.

Contents

Bullying Is Such Bull-oney

For the past 30 years, experts have done surveys with kids of all ages to get the scoop on bullying. The results show that bullying is a big, big, big problem in schools, neighborhoods, and communities. This is a problem not only in North America but in countries all over the world.

SURVEY SAYS

1 in 3 students are bullied during the school year

1 in 3 students bully someone

Nearly 9 out of 10 students have been "bystanders"

What is a *bystander*? Any person who sees bullying or knows about it. The person might stand by and allow bullying to continue. Or he or she might help one of the people involved—the person bullying or the person being bullied.

Maybe you watched someone being bullied and you wanted to help but didn't know how. Maybe you were scared you'd become a target, too. Perhaps the bullying and your own behavior bothered you later on, and you felt sad, angry, guilty, or confused.

Experts now know:

> Bystanders are hurt just as much by bullying as the people who are bullied. In fact, everyone involved in bullying is hurt by it, even the people who do the bullying. If you watch bullying but don't help, you're more likely to have stress, worry, and anger. Studies have shown that students who see and hear "violent interactions" (like bullying) are more likely to dislike school or even avoid it.

Some kids feel as if they have no power. But guess what? You *do* have power. You aren't helpless, but you need to know *how* to help. This book shows you how to stop bullying in a safe, confident way.

- If you've been a bystander, you'll learn to take a stand and lend a hand.

- If you've been bullied, you'll learn that kids care and can help.

- If you've bullied others, you'll see that you're not a bad person. You have done mean things—but you can change.

While everyone can be hurt by bullying, **bystanders have more power to stop bullying than anyone else.** More power than teachers. More power than parents. More power than the Principal of the Universe, whoever that is.

You know that awful feeling you get when someone is being bullied? That twisting in your stomach? You get that feeling because you know bullying is wrong. But when you use your power to help stop bullying, that feeling changes. It becomes a *good* feeling. In fact, it feels GREAT.

What does *power* mean? It doesn't mean big muscles or loud race cars. It means the ability to change things—and you have it, whether you realize it or not.

The goal of this book is to help you use your power to take a bite out of the bullying bull-oney.

Chapter 1

Have you Heard the (Bad) News?

A lot of people are talking about bullying: teachers, principals, parents, counselors, reporters—even celebrities. They're speaking out about how bullying happens on school playgrounds and in classrooms, cafeterias, hallways, and bathrooms. They're saying the bullying has to stop.

You know who's not talking so much about bullying? Kids.

The kids who get bullied are often afraid to speak up.

The kids who do the bullying sure don't want to admit it—at least not to adults.

And the kids who see the bullying? Most of them aren't talking either.

But with your help, this can change! First, you have to know what bullying is.

What *Is* Bullying?

Bullying – Bullying occurs when someone *repeatedly* and *purposely* hurts or scares another person.

The person doing the bullying has some type of *advantage* over the target (such as size or popularity).

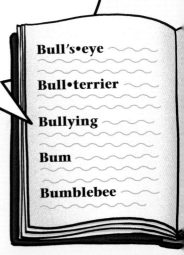

Bull's•eye

Bull•terrier

Bullying

Bum

Bumblebee

The Many Faces of Bullying

Physical bullying means someone uses his or her body to hurt, scare, or get control over another person. Examples: *hitting, kicking, tripping, pushing and pulling, holding someone down, grabbing, spitting, poking, blocking paths, giving "wedgies," putting someone's head in a toilet, throwing things, pulling hair, biting, scratching*

Experts now know that boys physically bully more than girls do.

As you probably know, a hurt body leads to hurt feelings inside.

Verbal bullying is when someone uses words to hurt others. Mean comments are made about someone's looks, clothes, behavior, interests, family, ethnic background, religion, or disability. Verbal bullying includes: *yelling, saying or whispering cruel words, swearing, laughing at someone, making mean phone calls*

Boys and girls do verbal bullying equally.

You know the old saying, "Sticks and stones may break my bones but names will never hurt me"? Bullied kids know that it's just plain wrong. Verbal bullying may not hurt the body—but it sure hurts feelings.

Relational bullying happens when someone tries to damage a person's relationship with friends and peers. Examples: *spreading lies, gossip, and rumors; ignoring someone; ganging up; not letting someone join in; telling the person's secrets; telling others not to hang out with him or her*

Both boys and girls do relational bullying, but girls do it more often.

This type of bullying is especially hurtful, because it can prevent someone from having friends and can make them feel embarrassed, excluded, and depressed.

Cyberbullying is when people use computers and cell phones to harass others. They may type nasty messages or send embarrassing pictures through cell phones or in emails, websites, chat rooms, blogs, message boards, online polling sites, and instant messages. They might pretend they're someone else online, share private information without permission, and trick people into telling their passwords. They might also leave certain people out by ignoring them in chats or making sure no one responds to their messages on message boards.

Both girls and boys cyberbully.

1 in 5 students are cyberbullied. 1 in 5 students cyberbully.

Kids who are cyberbullied say it's just as painful as face-to-face bullying (if not more so).

Bullying Isn't . . .

. . . the same as a little teasing or kidding around. Someone might say:

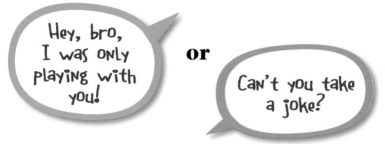

People think saying stuff like that gives them a "free pass" to bully. It doesn't!

Remember, bullying is when someone *repeatedly* does something *on purpose* to hurt or bother someone else. The person doing it has an advantage over the person he or she targets and uses that advantage to cause harm.

Teasing crosses over the line into bullying when the target gets hurt and wants the words or actions to stop—but they keep on coming. The teasing continues, even if the target is crying or saying, "Stop!"

This is VERY DIFFERENT from playful teasing between friends. If a friend says, "You're such a klutz" when you fall down—but is smiling and helping you up—the words are meant to poke a little fun at you. Your friend cares about you and is simply kidding around.

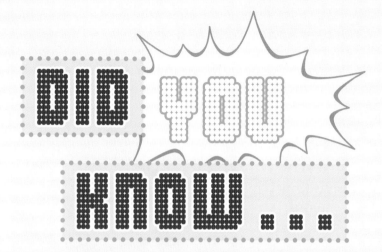

. . . that people usually get bullied because of their differences? Someone makes fun of their race, religion, or family background. Or someone makes fun of the way they look or act. But *everyone* is different in some way—and that's a *good* thing!

Many kids are bullied at some point during the school years. If you've been bullied, you are not alone. Even if you have escaped bullying in the past, it may catch up to you tomorrow, the next day, or sometime this school year. When you help kids who are bullied, you not only help *them* but you also help yourself. Why? Because there's only *one* way to prevent anyone from being bullied: be a part of ending bullying! The more kids who stand up, the sooner this will happen.

Well, you've read a lot of *bad* news—how about some *good* news? The good news is that the next chapter has games.

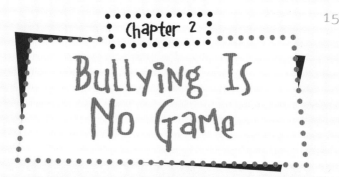

Chapter 2
Bullying Is No Game

Sometimes it can seem like kids who bully are "playing games" with you. They do and say *what* they want, *when* they want, according to their own set of rules. (Unfair rules!) At times, you may feel like a "pawn" in a game of chess.

Pawns are the little guys on the chess board, the ones who seem to have no power. But guess what? Pawns *do* have power. In chess, a pawn can cross the entire board a square at a time. When that happens, the pawn can become as powerful as any other piece on the board—without being mean!

This book shows you how to take the steps and claim your power.

But first, how about some games?

"Eye Spy" Bullying

Directions: Use the clues on the next page to keep your eye on bullying.

Eye spy a **mean message** and a **rude look,**
one kid **stealing** another's book,
a wad of gum on someone's chair,
spitballs landing in **someone's hair,**
a **bullied kid** who's about to fall . . .
and a **guinea pig who sees it all.**

Tic Tac Toe ■■■■■■■■■■■■■■■■■■■■■

Directions: True statements and myths are mixed into the board on page 19. (A myth is an *invented story* or an *unproved false belief*.) **Put an X on top of the myths and an O on top of the truths. See if you can find three in a row!**

(Photocopy the page or cut out little Xs and Os from notebook paper to place over the clues.)

Hint: A total of 4 TRUTHS and 5 MYTHS are on the board.

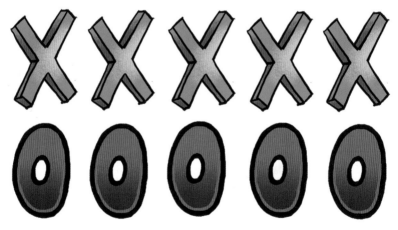

Answers: Three truths in a row can be found in Column 1 going down (green, orange, blue). Three myths in a row can be found in Column 3 going down (brown, pink, yellow). But two other myths and one truth are left! In Column 2 going down: red is a myth, purple is a truth, and gray is a myth.

Busters

Arm yourself with facts so you can bust these myths about bullying.

Myth #1: Bullying only affects a few kids.

FACT: If you had one dollar for each bullied kid, you'd be a millionaire—43 times! That's right. Studies show that nearly 43 million kids are bullied at some point during their school years.

Myth #2: Some kids deserve to be bullied.

FACT: Talk like this makes people think bullying is okay. Hurting others is never okay. No one deserves to be treated poorly. Even saying that *some* people deserve to be bullied is a myth. Instead of thinking about *some,* think about *all. All* people deserve respect. (Read more about respect on page 56.)

Myth #3: Bullied kids should fight back.

FACT: Bullying usually gets worse and lasts longer when kids physically fight back. Trying to fight someone means you could get hurt or get in trouble—even if you're defending yourself.

(What should you do instead? See pages 93–112 for ideas.)

Myth #4: Teachers always know when bullying occurs.

FACT: Kids who bully hide their "dirty work" from teachers. They often wait until teachers and other adults are out of the way or not looking, so they're less likely to get caught.

Myth #5: Kids who bully are cool.

FACT: Nope—anyone who bullies is *cruel*. It's mean to boss around other kids, scare them, hurt them, or make them feel invisible. Bullying is NOT proof that someone is powerful or popular. (Even if the person *seems* popular, it's never cool to be cruel.)

Bullying myths are dangerous. Why? Because false information keeps bullying alive. Sort of like the walking dead.

Truth Finders

Truth #1: Bullying happens in schools every day.

Imagine you are in a group with three friends. Each day, one of you could be bullied. That's right, one out of four kids (25 percent) are bullied *every day* in schools.

Truth #2: The damage from bullying can last a long time.

You may see bullying happen and think it's over when it ends. The bullying might be over but not the hurting. People involved in bullying can suffer from hurt feelings or injuries years after the bullying stops— even the person who did the bullying. Even a person who just *witnessed* the bullying.

Truth #3: Unstopped, bullying will continue.

Some kids won't stop bullying unless they hit a "roadblock." (Meaning someone stops them.) Children who bully and never change their ways usually grow into adults who bully. They then bully their kids, spouses, parents, coworkers, and other adults.

Truth #4: Some adults bully.

People of all shapes, sizes, and ages can bully. Even *teachers* can pick on kids. That's messed up! Don't think it's okay because they're adults. Bullying is never okay. Tell an adult you trust *immediately* if teachers, parents, or other adults bully. Bullying is wrong no matter who does it.

The TRUTH is powerful. It rules!

Don't Let Bullying Put You in Jeopardy

It's a sad fact: Many people are bullied. If someone chooses *you* to bully, it doesn't mean you're a "dork" or "loser." And it *doesn't* mean you deserve it.

In fact, some of the most successful people in the world were targeted by the meanest of the mean when they were younger. These people didn't just survive after going through rough times. They went on to accomplish great things.

Directions: Photocopy the game board on pages 26–27 and look at the clues. Can you guess the name of the bullied celeb? Write your answers on your photocopied page next to each hint. Then go to pages 28–29 to see the filled-in game board. How many did you get right?

FAMOUS PEOPLE

SINGERS

This popular Canadian singer was no "baby" about being bullied on the Internet.

This pop singer didn't understand why darker-skinned classmates cursed her lighter-colored skin.

Fans go "gaga" over this singer who was bullied because she had a "big nose" and "buck teeth."

He wanted to "Beat It" (get out of there) when his father bullied him.

ACTORS AND ACTRESSES

This actress and singer may rock at camp, but students at her school signed a "We all hate [name]" petition.

His school days got "hairy" when he landed the Harry role and his peers became jealous.

This young actress didn't get lost in the "Twilight" even though kids were mean to her.

This British born "vampire" was repeatedly beaten up at school. Today he'd like to take a bite out of bullying.

WHO WERE BULLIED

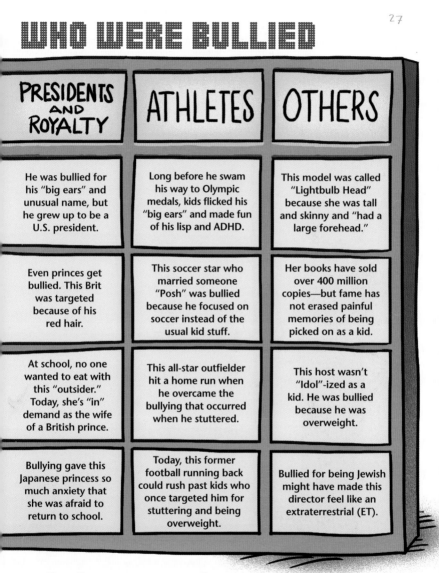

PRESIDENTS AND ROYALTY

He was bullied for his "big ears" and unusual name, but he grew up to be a U.S. president.

Even princes get bullied. This Brit was targeted because of his red hair.

At school, no one wanted to eat with this "outsider." Today, she's "in" demand as the wife of a British prince.

Bullying gave this Japanese princess so much anxiety that she was afraid to return to school.

ATHLETES

Long before he swam his way to Olympic medals, kids flicked his "big ears" and made fun of his lisp and ADHD.

This soccer star who married someone "Posh" was bullied because he focused on soccer instead of the usual kid stuff.

This all-star outfielder hit a home run when he overcame the bullying that occurred when he stuttered.

Today, this former football running back could rush past kids who once targeted him for stuttering and being overweight.

OTHERS

This model was called "Lightbulb Head" because she was tall and skinny and "had a large forehead."

Her books have sold over 400 million copies—but fame has not erased painful memories of being picked on as a kid.

This host wasn't "Idol"-ized as a kid. He was bullied because he was overweight.

Bullied for being Jewish might have made this director feel like an extraterrestrial (ET).

For the answers, turn the page!

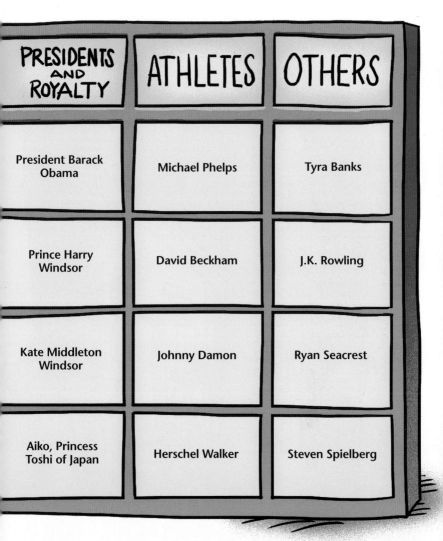

PRESIDENTS AND ROYALTY	ATHLETES	OTHERS
President Barack Obama	Michael Phelps	Tyra Banks
Prince Harry Windsor	David Beckham	J.K. Rowling
Kate Middleton Windsor	Johnny Damon	Ryan Seacrest
Aiko, Princess Toshi of Japan	Herschel Walker	Steven Spielberg

These superstars might not have been
bullied if bystanders had stood up for them.

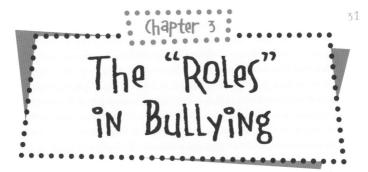

Chapter 3

The "Roles" in Bullying

Bullying might seem pretty simple: Someone hurts someone else over and over again. *Ouch!*

But bullying is more complicated than that. You know that people can do harm with their words and actions. You may be dealing with this now. In "Bullying Is No Game," you learned that a person who bullies can be any age and can hurt all sorts of people. You also discovered many myths and truths about bullying.

The biggest truth of all is that bullying is wrong. Bullying isn't simple, because the people involved in it play different roles. This chapter will help you see those roles in a new way.

"Another Bad Day" (A Very Short Play)

ACT ONE
(Abby's
bedroom.)

ABBY: I wish alarm clocks and buses and school had never been invented!

MOM: Abby, hurry up or you'll be late.

ABBY: My stomach hurts! I can't go to school today! Or ever again.

MOM: Honey, the doctor says you're fine. Why don't you try to go to school? I bet you'll feel better as the day goes on.

ABBY: No one understands!

ACT TWO
(The bus stop. Abby doesn't like what she sees.)

ABBY: Oh, great, there's "Bullying Billy-Bob" picking on Victor again.

BILLY-BOB JENKINS: Yo, Victor, you're so fat you take up a whole movie theater! Do they charge you for one ticket or a hundred?

VICTOR: *(Head hanging.)* Leave me alone.

THE TWISTED TWINS: *(Laughing with Billy-Bob, egging him on.)* Dude, that's hilarious!

ABBY: *(Whispers to herself.)* Same old story.

BILLY-BOB JENKINS: Hey, Victor, I'll help you go on a diet, 'cause your body fat could keep you alive for a year! Give me your lunch.

VICTOR: *(He holds his lunch bag tighter.)* No, it's mine.

BILLY-BOB JENKINS: *(He grabs the lunch bag, finds some chocolate milk, and pours it down Victor's shirt.)* Oh, look, Mommy packed you a *chocowat miwk.* Isn't that sweet! Yeah, it's yours all right—and now it's all over you! You should have worn a bib, you big baby!

THE TWISTED TWINS: *(They laugh and cheer as if they're at a sports event.)* What a slob! Try not to cry, baby!

ABBY: *(She starts to get a headache. She sees the bus but doesn't feel relieved. She knows "Bullying Billy-Bob" will keep bugging Victor all the way to school. She wants to say something—but when she opens her mouth, all that comes out is a squeak.)*

BILLY-BOB JENKINS: You say something, "Mousey"? I didn't *think* so.

Who Plays What?

In the play you just read:

Victor is the **target**, or the person who is bullied.

Billy-Bob is the **bully**—the person who makes the target's life miserable.

Abby is a **bystander**. She *witnesses*—or sees—the bullying.

What about the Twisted Twins? People who encourage bullying by cheering or laughing are **reinforcers**. They "reinforce"—strengthen or support—bullying through their actions.

Surprising Fact:
Reinforcers are also
bystanders.

According to experts, bystanders can also be:

- **Outsiders:** They watch the bullying, up close or from a distance, but do nothing. In the play you've been reading, Abby is an outsider.

- **Assistants:** They help the bullying by holding down the target or acting as a lookout. They might push, pull, or hit the bullied person, too.

- **Upstanders:** They stand up and speak out against the bullying.

As you can see, bystanders aren't just kids who stand around watching. Sometimes, they increase the violence by *helping it happen*.

And sometimes they can stop it. (More on this soon.)

Terms like *bully* and *target* help people understand the different roles in bullying. But these words only refer to a person's role at the time of the bullying. They *don't* say anything about who a person *really* is. That's why it's best never to call someone a name like "bully." When someone is labeled, it's easy to see the person only as the label, but not see the person inside.

Plus, labels can stick even though people may change. For example, a kid who bullies for years can change and decide to be kind. If you've helped someone bully, that doesn't mean that you're glued to that role forever.

A Tell-the-Truth Quiz

Answer **T** (True) or **F** (False) about what you've learned so far.

T or **F**? **Outsiders** are people who act like a trio of monkeys—they see nothing, hear nothing, and say nothing.

T or **F**? **Assistants** like to play games. Their favorite is "Follow the Leader." Their second favorite is "Trouble."

T or **F**? **Reinforcers** act like cheerleaders for the person who bullies. (So maybe they should carry fluffy pom-poms everywhere they go!)

T or **F**? **Reinforcers** are like parrots—they repeat what bullies say.

T or **F**? Being an **Outsider** is like stepping in dog poo—it stinks to be there!

A Personal Question

Have you ever taken the role of . . .

Chances are, you've played many of these different roles at different times in your life—maybe even on the same day. It's okay if you've taken on these roles in the past. This book is about what you decide to do now and in the future. It can help you make changes and learn to play the part of an **Upstander!** (For more on that, see pages 58–59.)

A Happy Ending?

Can Victor be a *victor*? (If you didn't read the play on pages 32–34, go back and check it out. Get some popcorn, if you want.)

The curtain rises . . .

ACT THREE
(In the classroom. Abby walks quickly to her desk and sits down with arms crossed. Tears fill her eyes.)

MS. FRIZZ: *(Walks over to Abby's desk.)* What's wrong, Abby?

ABBY: *(She sees Billy-Bob, the Twisted Twins, Victor, and the rest of the class watching. Abby doesn't want to be called a tattletale.)* Nothing.

MS. FRIZZ: Can I speak to you in the hallway, please?

BILLY-BOB JENKINS: *(Whispers as Abby walks past his desk.)* Keep your mouth shut—or else.

MS. FRIZZ: Abby, please tell me what's bothering you. You've been having a hard time for more than a month, and I want to help.

ABBY: *(Abby doesn't want to say anything, but the words fly out of her mouth.)* Billy-Bob keeps bullying Victor. I want to stop it, but I don't know what to do! I'm afraid he'll bully me if I say anything, so I just stand there!

MS. FRIZZ: *(Puts her hand on Abby's shoulder.)* I'm glad you told me this, Abby. When people don't say anything about bullying, they allow it to continue. Staying silent is almost like giving someone permission to hurt others. What you're doing now is being an *Upstander.* An Upstander acts to stop bullying. I know it's scary and it takes a lot of courage to speak up, but I'll make sure that you and Victor are safe. I'll set up a meeting so we can talk more about ways you and your friends can become Upstanders.

ABBY: Thanks, Ms. Frizz. I hope you're right about this.

ACT FOUR
(Next day at the bus stop. After hearing the word *Upstanders*, Abby is feeling more confident.)

BILLY-BOB JENKINS: *(Grinning, he walks toward Victor and shoves him.)* Hey, "Lunchroom"! What's on the menu today? Give me your lunch bag.

ABBY: *(Before Billy-Bob can take Victor's lunch, Abby steps in.)* We can walk to the other bus stop down the street, Victor. And Billy-Bob, you need to chill.

BILLY-BOB JENKINS: *(He has a startled look on his face. He's surprised Abby spoke, and more surprised she's standing up for Victor after all this time.)* Butt out, "Big Mouth."

THE TWISTED TWINS: *(They stand on either side of Billy-Bob and laugh meanly.)* Abby's mouth is as big as Victor's butt! Those two must be in LOVE!

ABBY: *(Victor and Abby are now halfway down the block.)* Victor, you need to tell Bullying Billy-Bob to leave you alone.

VICTOR: I can't. He'll beat me up. But thanks anyway.

ABBY: You *can* do something to stop the bullying. And I'm tired of being scared of Billy-Bob. I talked to Ms. Frizz and my mom and dad. It's time for us to take a stand.

VICTOR: *(Thinks about it.)* Abby, did you see how Bullying Billy-Bob froze for a second when you told him to chill? You took him by surprise. If I knew I had some other people backing me up, I think I could stand up to him.

ABBY: *(She and Victor reach the next stop, where a few kids from their school wait for the bus.)* Here's our chance to get some backup. Let's see what they say . . .

VICTOR: *(Confides in the kids at the bus stop, with Abby's help.)* He just won't leave me alone. But I'm ready to face him, if you guys will help me.

BUS STOP KID: If we say anything, Billy-Bob will bully us.

ABBY: And if you don't do anything, he will probably bully you anyway. Last month he picked on Tanya. This month it's Victor. Next month it could be any of us.

BUS STOP KID: I don't know . . .

VICTOR: Billy-Bob can't bully us if we show him we're united, because there's too many of us to go after. Plus, together we have mega-power.

BUS STOP KIDS: *(Agree to help.)*

BILLY-BOB JENKINS: *(He and the twins walk up to Victor and get in his face.)* Don't stand here. The sidewalk will crack.

VICTOR: *(Stands tall. Feels stronger when Abby and the others gather round him. He looks in Billy-Bob's eyes.)* Lay off, Billy-Bob. Bullying isn't cool. It hurts people. It's time for you to stop.

BILLY-BOB JENKINS: *(Angry, he makes his hands into fists. He notices the Twisted Twins aren't laughing now. They look nervous.)* Oh yeah, who's gonna stop me?

ABBY: *(Takes a step forward.)* I will!

BUS STOP KIDS: We will!

VICTOR: And I will, too.

BILLY-BOB JENKINS: *(He sees that the twins have backed away.)* Fine. Whatever. See if we care. We're outta here.

BUS STOP KIDS: All right!

VICTOR: Wow, I can't believe that worked! Thanks, Abby. Thanks, *everyone!*

We Interrupt This Program for Some Breaking News

When kids intervene—meaning they *get involved* and *give help*—bullying **STOPS**

in **10 seconds or less**

more than half of the time!

That means kids like YOU have the power to stop bullying . . .

and that's no **bull-oney.**

Chapter 4

Upstanders, Unite!

Maybe you're thinking: "Why should I get involved if I see someone getting bullied? It's not my business. In fact, I've been told to stay out of other people's business!"

Good point.

But . . .

. . . when it comes to bullying, it *is* your business—even if you're not the one being bullied. The violence affects you. How? Think about it this way . . . have you ever:

- felt helpless when you've seen friends hurt by bullying?

- felt guilty because you didn't speak up about bullying?

- been afraid of becoming someone's next target?

- gotten angry about the bullying you've witnessed?

- felt powerless to stop the bullying?

Or have you ever said, "Phew! I'm glad there's no school on Saturday"?*

*Thought so.

The bullying you witness is like a monkey on your back. Not a cute little monkey. A big, fat, hairy monkey with bad teeth. It's a pain in the back. And it weighs you down.

Bullying Makes School *Harder*

How can you focus at school if you have to keep looking over your shoulder trying to avoid someone who might bully you?

How can you use the school bathroom if it's not a bully-free place?

And how can your teacher get through the science lesson if he spends the whole class trying to pry Angela's butt off the chair that Marco put Mega-Glue on?

Maybe you miss out on the science lesson.

Then you flunk the test.

So your grandma refuses to buy you that new video game you wanted.

It could happen!

At school, you have the right to *learn* and *feel safe*. Everybody does.

You also have a responsibility to your classmates and school. It's your duty as a student to help others when they're being hurt. Standing up for others means you're doing the right thing. (And you don't have to do it alone.)

The Respect Connection

Being an Upstander is about respecting others. What is *respect*? When you respect people, you care about their feelings, thoughts, ideas, likes, wants, needs, and dreams. You value each person as a human being.

When you show respect for others, you don't judge them, make fun of them, or hurt them. You include others, instead of excluding them. You notice others, instead of ignoring them. And you don't bully!

The great thing about respect is that when you give it, it often comes right back.

Upstanders are respect role models.

1. They respect others and themselves.
2. They encourage others to do the same.
3. They help spread peace and cooperation.
4. They notice disrespect and bullying.
5. They lend a hand to people who are bullied.

How to Be an Upstander

Being an Upstander starts with one person who wants to right a wrong. (Bullying is the wrong.)

You can be that person!

Upstanders have certain qualities in common. They're:

- **Caring**—they think about other people's wants and needs.

- **Empathetic**—they think about other people's feelings.

- **Helpful**—they like to be of service to others.

- **Kind** and **giving**—they do nice things for other people because it feels good inside.

- **Brave**—they take a stand, even if they're scared to do so.

- **Risk-takers**—they're willing to take a positive risk to help someone out.

If you have some of these qualities, that's great. If you don't have them today, that's okay. You can have them tomorrow! How? One way is to copy characteristics you admire in others. Another is to visualize (imagine) yourself with those qualities.

Each one of us can make changes for the better. It starts with you. Then other people might notice and follow in your footsteps. You can lead the Upstander march! If you know other Upstanders, you can join them.

Y U Need 2 Unite

The more Upstanders there are in a school, the more power they have against bullying. It's sort of like forming a kickball team. You would lose if you only had one or two players. The more players you have, the stronger your team. If you have nine players and a bench full of substitutes supporting your efforts, then you have a great shot at winning.

Your goal as a group of Upstanders is to stand up to bullying and let bullied kids know you're looking out for them.

How can you get others to become Upstanders? You could promise them you'll do their homework every night. (Kidding!) Or you could use your noodle* and explain why standing up is better than standing by.

*Your head!

Stand Up Because . . .

- *Anyone* could become the next target. No one is completely safe from bullying.

- Bullying hurts *everyone*, including those who stand by and watch.

- Studies show that most kids want bullying to end. Studies also show that *kids* have the power to end bullying.

- There are many safe and successful ways for kids to stand up to bullying. (You can read about them on pages 69–91.)

When you're ready to find kids to join you as Upstanders, start with your best friends—these are the people you trust the most and who are more likely to support you. Help them understand that bullying is as uncool as a bowl of sweat-sock soup.

In other words: not cool at all.

Cool is

helping people

being kind to them

treating others
with respect

Cool is . . . ice cream. If you "lick" bullying, you'll have a great taste in your mouth.

Suppose your friends agree that bullying should be stopped? Great! *But* your friends may still have doubts about getting involved . . .

Maybe they:

- are afraid of getting bullied. (Tell them: You're safer in a group because members defend each other.)

- believe reporting someone for bullying is "tattling." (Tell them: It's not. Tattling is trying to get someone INto trouble, while reporting gets people OUT of trouble.)

- think they don't have the power to stop bullying. (Tell them: Bystanders have power! It's been proven over and over—bystanders can stop bullying. That's what this book is about!)

- worry they might lose friends at school. (Tell them: When bystanders join together, they *make* friends with other bystanders and those they've helped. You might lose a friendship with a person who bullies, but would you want to be friends with someone who hurts people?)

Tell them:

When we work together, we increase our power.

Learn more about "POWER" on pages 69–91.

Helping Grownups Stand Up

Kids can do a good job standing up to bullying, but the work will be easier if adults help, too. Talk to the grownups at school about working together to put an end to bullying. A good place to begin is with your teacher. You can photocopy the "10 Ways Adults Can Join the Upstander Team" on pages 66–67 and give it to the adults at school (teachers, the principal, a school counselor or social worker, school aides, a custodian, a school nurse, other specialists, parent volunteers, bus drivers, and so on).

Bullying doesn't only happen in the classroom and at school, though. It happens everywhere kids gather. So share the list with every adult who works with children. Give a copy to your club leaders or team coaches. Show it to your Boy/Girl Scout, 4-H, Camp Fire USA, YMCA/YWCA, or religious group leaders. If you go to an after-school program or summer camp, bring copies for the adults there, too.

Ten Ways Adults Can Join the Upstander Team

1. Teach about bullying. Show how it hurts kids, and suggest ways that all students can help end bullying.

2. Stop bullying incidents immediately. Give fair consequences that will prevent future bullying.

3. Develop a bullying survey to help students find out more about bullying in their class and school.

4. Read fiction and nonfiction stories about bullying. Assign a bullying book report. (How did bullying affect the characters? What did any bystanders do? Were their actions positive or negative?)

5. Ask the class to interview people about their experiences with bullying and then give a written or an oral report. For example, they might ask other kids if they've been bullied, how it felt, and what they did to stop the bullying. They might ask family members to recount bullying incidents from their lives or to tell about the role bystanders played at school.

6. Create an anti-bullying newsletter. Ask students to brainstorm ideas to stop bullying, and include them as tips. Or, report the ideas over the school loudspeaker or on school television during morning announcements. Put it on your class or school website.

7. Write a class play in which Upstanders use different strategies to stop bullying.

8. Role-play bullying situations where Upstanders step in. Let students act out the different roles (the "bully," the "target," "bystanders," "Upstanders"). This encourages empathy and allows students to practice anti-bullying skills.

9. Ask the principal to have a school-wide (or grade-wide) "Upstander Day." Each class or grade must come up with an Upstander "Plan of Action." For example, create a buddy program where kids become friends with kids who have been bullied. Or make anti-bullying bracelets to create an atmosphere that supports kids who are bullied.

10. Praise and reward student Upstanders. (But when discussing bullying, tell kids not to use real names of kids who bully or are targeted.) Examples:

    - Certificates for Upstander activities, given during class or in special assemblies
    - "Upstander of the Week" award
    - Recognition of Upstanders and their actions during circle time or class discussions
    - "Upstander Hall of Fame" list for school bulletin boards
    - Prize box (stickers, pencils, bookmarks)
    - Extra free time during school
    - Privileges (such as line or group leader), because Upstanders are leaders!

When kids report bullying, follow through. Know and follow your school or organization's procedures. If your school could do a better job preventing and responding to bullying, work with others to make that happen.

Chapter 5

Upstanders Have POWER

Part of the reason people bully is because they think hurting others makes them stronger. They feel even more powerful when other kids watch the bullying but don't stop it, or when kids act as if bullying is "cool." When you don't stand up to bullying, you help make it worse and worse. It's almost like growing a Bully Monster—a bullying problem that gets *bigger and harder to handle* unless people work together to put an end to it.

If you say nothing, the bullying continues. The longer you stay around, the longer bullying lasts. And if you join in, the bullying becomes rougher.

OR

You can use your bystander power to prevent bullying from happening or to stop it in action. Instead of standing by, help tame that Bully Monster! (Otherwise known as the BM.)

Upstanders are part of a special group—can you guess what that group might be? Here are the clues:

Clue #1 They stand up for what's right.

Clue #2 They notice mean, dangerous, or violent situations.

Clue #3 They help keep people safe.

Clue #4 They show courage.

Clue #5 They have developed some special skills and powers.

Clue #6 They help make the world a better place.

In case you haven't figured out the answer yet, here's one final clue:

They

Help
EveryONe
Respect
Others

An Upstander is a . . .

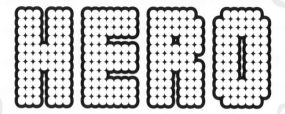

HERO

A hero is someone who knows it's wrong to hurt others and who tries to do the right thing.

This chapter will help you find your hero power. You'll learn how to:

Play With and Include Everyone

Object to Bullying

Walk Away Bravely

Escape (Have a Plan)

Request Help

When you unleash the power, your actions put the

on bullying.

Play With and Include Everyone

Kids usually don't pick on kids who have friends, because friends stand up for each other. To be an Upstander, include more kids in your activities and get to know them as friends.

Who are some kids you could invite to join you? Look for . . .

1. Kids who are alone a lot. Say hi or introduce yourself to kids you notice sitting, playing, or walking by themselves. Invite them to sit with you at lunch or play with you at recess. Like this:

- "Hi, I'm [name]. What's your name?"

- "There's an extra seat at our table. Come on over!"

- "We need some more kids for our game. Can we count you in?"

2. **Kids you can walk with.** Invite kids to walk with you to school, class, lunch, recess, and gym, or back home. Sticking together not only keeps you safe but also helps you find more friends. It's a good idea to avoid areas where you know bullying happens: unsupervised hallways, locker rooms, and bathrooms, or deserted areas on the school grounds.

3. **Kids who are new to your class.** Go up to a new student and introduce yourself. Or, get to know people you usually don't spend much time with. Ask kids to come over after school (with a parent's permission) or to join a club you belong to.

4. **Kids who have a hard time with social skills.** If some kids in your class seem to have difficulty getting along in social situations, you could help. Show them ways to be more confident or make friends. Sometimes, helping someone is as simple as reminding him or her to smile more, say hello, listen, take turns, share, stay calm, and be a good sport. (Be careful not to make kids feel bad, though. Focus on positive things they can do, not on the things you think they're doing wrong. Helpful: "People will like playing with you more if you follow the game rules." Not helpful: "Nobody wants to play with you because you always cheat.")

Object to Bullying

When kids bully, they often think that other kids "agree" with their words and actions because no one says otherwise. Let those kids know that what they do is wrong.

The tips in this section can help if you're the one being bullied or if you're an Upstander. It's all about staying strong in front of the person bullying you and letting him or her know that bullying isn't okay.

DO:

Use body language to act confident. (Even if you don't feel that way.) You can be nervous and scared inside, but try not to show it on the outside.

Bully-busting body language

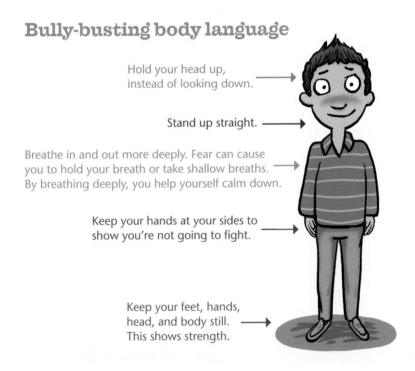

Hold your head up, instead of looking down.

Stand up straight.

Breathe in and out more deeply. Fear can cause you to hold your breath or take shallow breaths. By breathing deeply, you help yourself calm down.

Keep your hands at your sides to show you're not going to fight.

Keep your feet, hands, head, and body still. This shows strength.

Ignore the person bullying you. People bully to get a reaction—they want to see you get scared and upset. If you don't show fear, the person might stop. Sometimes, you might ignore bullying by getting busy with an activity.

But if the person bullying you sees your hands shaking or senses your fear, he or she will probably try to get a reaction out of you. Ignore the bullying, but make sure your body language shows quiet strength.

If the person gets angry or starts hurting you, ignoring is not a good strategy. Choose another one.

Give an *assertive* response. Assertive doesn't mean aggressive, angry, or mean. Assertive means strong, clear, and powerful while *respecting* others. You can use the following ideas if you are a target of bullying or if you are being an Upstander for someone else. Speak in a firm voice that can be heard by the person who is bullying and by people nearby.

Strategies to try:

Kid: Here comes the world's biggest loser.
Target Response: Don't bother me!
Upstander Response: Leave him alone!
(People who bully don't expect a direct response like this. You're letting him or her know you don't want to be a target. Your loud-and-clear words might also attract the attention of a nearby adult.)

Kid: Your glasses are thick, and you're a dork.
Target Response: Yes, I see a lot better with my glasses.
Upstander Response: Lots of people wear glasses.
(The person can't argue as easily if you agree.)

Kid: You're number one on the "Ugliest People in the World" list.
Target Response: I don't care.
Upstander Response: Whatever.
(The person may think you aren't bothered by the words.)

Kid: Rejects like you don't belong here.
Target Response: Thanks for the warm welcome.
Upstander Response: Wow, wasn't that nice?
(Humor can lessen the tension.)

Kid: I'm going to beat you up.
Target Response: My teacher is expecting me now. I have to go.
Upstander Response: Come on, we need to get back to class.
(This gives you a reason to leave.)

The key to all these responses is that they tell the person who is bullying you that you're not affected by the bullying.

But you still have to be careful when dealing with anyone who bullies!

DON'T:

- Show you are upset. (You don't want the other person to think he or she hurt your feelings.)

- Argue. (People who bully always think they're right.)

- Stare at the person or make a fist. (That's aggressive body language.)

- Try to hold on to money or belongings that a "bully" asks for. (Giving up your valuables is safer than getting hurt, and you might be able to get your stuff back after you tell an adult.)

- Get into a fight. (Remember, people who bully have an *advantage* such as physical strength or size over their targets. It's more important to keep yourself safe from harm.)

- Bring a weapon to defend yourself. (Someone could get seriously hurt and you could get in big trouble.)

Telling someone to stop being mean won't be in the top 10 on your favorite things to do list. (It might be the only time you would rather be cleaning your room!) But there *is* a secret to greater success and safety. Round up your friends and fellow Upstanders, and *together* tell the person who is bullying that you don't like bullying and want it to stop.

What can you say?

Bullying isn't cool.

Don't treat people that way.

Bullying isn't allowed in our school.

You're bullying, and you need to stop it.

Show some respect.

We're standing up for the people you bully. Stop now.

This will help put the brakes on bullying!

(Remember not to call anyone names, like *bully*. Nobody deserves to be labeled.)

Walk Away Bravely

Kids who bully love audiences. They want to show off how cool they think they are. When they have an audience, they think they have support. They get the (wrong) idea that other people are entertained by the bullying or approve of it in some way.

Don't let them think that anymore. Walking away means the audience disappears—*poof!*

So, just LEAVE. A group of Upstanders leaving the scene sends a strong message to anyone who bullies.

Bullying usually stops when there is no one left to watch.

Report the bullying you witnessed. (Read more about this on page 88: "Request Help.")

When you stop "feeding" the Bully Monster, you weaken it. And walking away with the person who was bullied stops the bullying. That's Upstander power in action!

Escape (Have a Plan)

Staying far away from people who bully might work for a while. But these kids seem to smell bullying targets the way dogs sniff out juicy steaks. Here are three escape plans you can share with kids who are bullied. You might need to use them yourself, too.

1. If you're alone and worried about being bullied, catch up to a group of kids and tag along with them. People are less likely to follow you if there are others around to defend you. Or, stand in sight of adults. (For tips on telling adults about bullying, see page 88).

2. If someone who wants to bully you approaches, yell for someone you know or walk toward a group. Some kids back off when they're outnumbered.

3. Create a distraction to make your escape or to delay the person who is bullying until an adult arrives. Distractions can work when you're trying to defend someone, too.

You could say:

- "A teacher is on the way."

- "The principal knows what you're doing and is coming for you."

- "I heard they put video cameras around here to stop bullying."

- "Have you heard the joke about the student who ate his homework? The teacher said it was a piece of cake!" (A joke might take the person by surprise.)

The recess monitor is coming and she doesn't look happy.

What if one of your *friends* is bullying? You need to get out of the friendship if you think the person is dangerous to hang around, especially if you're working on being an Upstander. To give your friend a chance to change, you could say:

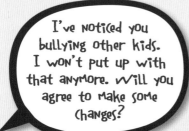

Request Help

This book is about trying to stop bullying on your own. Kids who decide to be Upstanders can make a big difference when it comes to ending bullying.

But not all bullying situations end quickly and easily. You may need adult help. When should you ask for assistance?

- If someone is having trouble getting out of a harmful situation

- If no one who is present can help

- If the bullying becomes dangerous

- If there are weapons or drugs

If you need an adult while bullying is happening, report the incident to the nearest adult you can find. Maybe that person is a lunchroom aide, a recess monitor, or a custodian. It could be teachers, coaches, the principal, the nurse, or a social worker or counselor.

You can also report bullying after the fact. You can tell an adult at school or home. You can even tell your doctor if you've been bullied or if you witness bullying. Grownups can help!

If you are worried about someone getting back at you for reporting, you can report anonymously. That means your name isn't used. Other ideas:

- Leave a note on your teacher's desk or in his or her school mailbox.

- Mail a letter about the bullying to your teacher or principal.

- Talk to your teacher before or after class, making sure nobody is around to see.

- Ask your parents or caregivers to call the school.

- Photocopy pages 66–67, "Ten Ways Adults Can Join the Upstander Team," and give it to your teacher.

- Ask a friend to help you tell an adult.

- Gather your group of Upstanders and report the bullying together as a team.

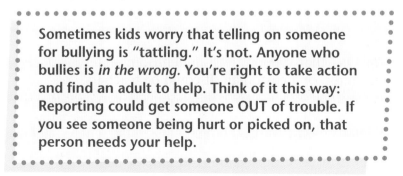

Sometimes kids worry that telling on someone for bullying is "tattling." It's not. Anyone who bullies is *in the wrong*. You're right to take action and find an adult to help. Think of it this way: Reporting could get someone OUT of trouble. If you see someone being hurt or picked on, that person needs your help.

Support Bullied Kids!

Spread the power by supporting kids who've been bullied. You can say:

Chapter 6

Ten Super Ways to Stand Up to Bullying

POWER (see pages 74–91) gives Upstanders five great ways to tackle bullying—but it's even more helpful to have a whole playbook full of ideas. Why? Just like in football, some plays work well in one situation but not as well in others. So, the bullying may be blocked with some strategies but not others. Sometimes, you might prefer one anti-bullying action to another. Knowledge about all the possible "plays" can help you become better at offense and defense. Score!

1. Follow the Golden Rule

The Golden Rule says, "Treat others the way you want to be treated." You don't want to be tripped, poked, or shoved. You don't want to be called names or excluded from activities. You don't want be bullied! So, make it a goal to treat other people with kindness and respect. To read more about respect, see page 56.

As an Upstander and HERO (see page 72), you can stand up for others. Then, if you're ever in a bad situation yourself, those same people might stand up for you!

2. Spread the Message

Kids often use the Internet to hurt people. But a HERO can use the Internet to *help* others! If you dislike bullying as much as you dislike eating Brussels sprouts, let others know. Send instant messages, texts, and emails to tell bullied kids you care about them and value them. For example:

IMO, U R GR8. IFYP. TTYL.

In other words: In my opinion (IMO), you (U) are (R) great (GR8). I feel your pain (IFYP). Talk to you later (TTYL).

Prevent cyberbullying by following these pointers.

DON'T:

- let kids talk you into cyberbullying

- send or forward hurtful instant messages, texts, or emails

- post anyone's secrets

- talk about other people in chat rooms

- share anyone's private information

- pretend you're someone else online

- vote on hate poll sites

- send embarrassing pictures

DO:

- tell kids who are bullied to:

  ⇨ log off

  ⇨ change their screen and IM names and email addresses

  ⇨ block anyone who cyberbullies

  ⇨ save hurtful IMs, texts, emails, or chats (for proof)

  ⇨ never respond or try to "get back at" people who bully

  ⇨ let adults know about the bullying

- tell your friends who cyberbully that it's wrong

- be as polite and thoughtful on the Internet as you are offline!

3. Wipe the Slate Clean

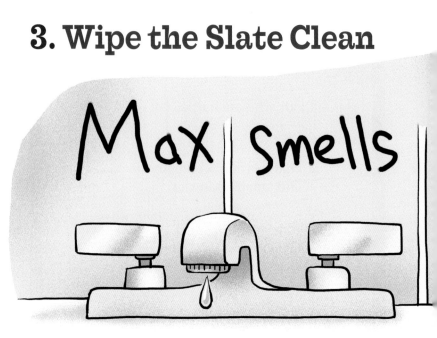

You might see *graffiti* like that on the bathroom walls at school, on desks and chairs, or on sidewalks. Did you know it's a form of bullying?

The words come from someone's marker instead of their mouth—but they hurt all the same. They harm the person being bullied and other people who read the messages, too.

What can you do if you see graffiti? Let a teacher or another adult at school know so it can get cleaned up right away.

It may be tempting to cross out the words, but that can make a bigger mess. At times, you may feel so angry about the mean messages that you want to write something back to the person who wrote it. But then *you're* doing graffiti—and you're bullying. It may be hard to treat someone who bullies with respect, but try to remember the Golden Rule. (See page 94.) Kindness can be contagious. If you're nice to people who bully, they may learn to be nice in return.

4. Tell It Like It Is

Maybe you've already told someone that you don't like his or her bullying. Maybe you've even tried to talk to the person about respect. Sometimes, people need to hear what could happen to them if they don't stop their behavior. Let them know how their actions can end up hurting *themselves*. You might say:

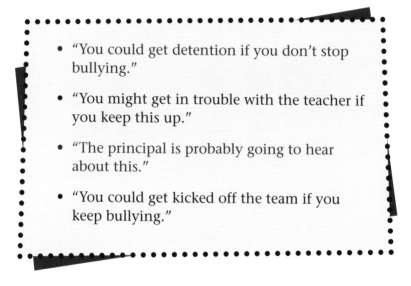

- "You could get detention if you don't stop bullying."

- "You might get in trouble with the teacher if you keep this up."

- "The principal is probably going to hear about this."

- "You could get kicked off the team if you keep bullying."

Another option is to privately tell the person who bullies:

> I think you're a good person under all the bullying you do...people would like you more if you'd be nicer.*

It may come as a surprise, but kids who bully are just kids like you. But some mistakenly believe that using power over others is a way to get what they want. Some are bullied at home, so they think it's okay or normal to hurt people. The good news is that they are *wrong* about all this. The extra good news is that bullying is a learned behavior. Why is that good? If something is learned, it can be *un*learned! People who bully can learn better ways to behave. They might even become buddies.

*Be sure to stay safe, though. See page 113.

5. Don't Let Adults Allow Bullying

Remember Truth #4—the one about how adults can bully, too? (See page 24.) Sometimes adults just stand by and watch kids bully other kids. Grownups have a responsibility to take action. It's their job to protect kids as best they can.

If an adult at your school knows about bullying and does nothing to stop it, it's the same as saying it's okay. It's almost like giving kids the go-ahead to go ahead and bully.

If you've seen this happen in the past and didn't know what to do, that's okay. But now you know that you *can* report this adult to another grownup you trust. For example, if a teacher at school doesn't stop a bullying incident, you can tell the principal. If a bus driver doesn't stop the bullying that happens on the bus, report this to your principal, too. Be sure to let your parents know about the issue as well. There are adults you can trust to do the right thing.

It's possible that your home is a place where bullying occurs. Who can you talk to about it? Find a trusted grownup: a relative, an adult friend of the family, your doctor, a school nurse, a school counselor, or your religious leader. Getting help is so important. It's scary to talk about issues like these, but it's a way to stand up for yourself and stay safe.

6. Buddy Up

Kids who are frequently bullied feel sad, hurt, lonely, and left out. They may also feel angry, frustrated, and confused. Maybe you often feel this way. Or maybe you know kids who do.

You know what can help? Having a friend. The support of just one person can make a difference!

Reach out to kids who are bullied. Get to know them better and try to become friends. Talk, play sports, or spend time together after school. Have fun! Maybe you and your new friends can write the world's shortest book: "Nice Things About Bullying." (It's zero pages long!)

If you know that someone has been bullied, show your support. Help the person let out feelings of hurt, anger, and sadness. Listening is helpful and shows you care. You could also encourage the person to talk to an adult for further help.

True Upstander Stories

David Shepherd and Travis Price came to the rescue of a student who was bullied for wearing pink to school. The boys gave their friends pink shirts and emailed everyone they knew asking them to dress in pink. The next day their school looked like a sea of pink! The kids who bullied weren't heard from again.

Ten-year-old Jaylen Arnold was bullied because of his Tourette syndrome. It makes his body twitch and causes him to make unwanted noises. Jaylen didn't want other kids to go through what he did, so he created a website about bullying. (It's called Jaylen's Challenge: www.jaylenschallenge.org.) He sells "Bullying No Way!" wristbands to raise money to spread the word about bullying awareness. Jaylen also has given school presentations to spread the word.

7. Get Involved

A HERO can become a leader and think of ways to stop bullying throughout the school. Here are some ideas that have worked for other kids:

- Draw anti-bullying posters and get permission to hang them in classrooms, in hallways, on school bulletin boards, and in the cafeteria.

- Older students can develop anti-bullying presentations. Show the harmful effects of bullying or safe ways to be an Upstander. Present the ideas to your class and school.

- Start an anti-bullying club. Brainstorm ways to stop bullying, using the ideas in this book. Support bullied kids by inviting them to join.

- Some schools have created a "Friendship Bench" for the playground. Adults and kids work together to build a bench that can be used by kids who are bullied, kids who want quiet time, or those who are looking for friends and peers to be social with.

- Survey students to find out more about the bullying taking place at your school. Share the results with your teachers and principal.

- With adult help, form an "Anti-Bullying Squad" that patrols the lunchroom, playground, hallways, and school grounds. The squad can be on the lookout for bullying. If they see someone being bullied, squad members can report this to an adult. The squad can also support bullied students by giving encouragement and friendship.

8. Say "No Way"

Saying no to kids who bully can sometimes feel as uncomfortable as sitting on a porcupine. But you can learn to say no and stick to that answer. It's easier if you practice your responses ahead of time. Try some of these:

Don't give in to peer pressure. Say no with confidence! (For tips on body language, see page 77.)

9. Don't Pass the Trash

Rumors occur when one person spreads gossip to another, who spreads it to another, who spreads it to another. Each person is a like a link on a chain that gets longer and longer. Often, the information in the rumor is untrue and could hurt the person it's about. As the rumor gets passed on through the chain of pain, there's hardly any truth left to it. People add details to make the gossip "more interesting."

Rumors and gossip can be a form of bullying. (See *relational bullying*, page 9.) You know what you can do to stop rumors? Refuse to pass the trash!

Face the person who's spreading rumors and gossip. Look him or her in the eye. Say something like, "I won't repeat anything that could hurt someone."

Let your friends and classmates know that you're not one to spread rumors. It's a sign of respect for others when you give up the gossip. It's also part of the Golden Rule (see page 94).

10. Take Away Power from People Who Bully

People who bully aren't picky. You qualify for their "Kids to Bully" list if you breathe and have a heartbeat. *No one* is safe from bullying. Kids part a path when kids who bully walk down the hall. It's not because they farted.

But you and other Upstanders can take the power out of bullying by letting kids know that no one supports people who hurt others.

Upstanders can stand strong as a group and say:

- "We will only be your friend if you stop bullying!" (High fives all around.)

- "We're going to let a teacher know what you're doing." (Then report the bullying.)

- "Booooo! Not cool!" (Do this when anyone makes fun of others.)

- "We want a bully-free school!" (Everyone can applaud afterward.)

That's called making your voices heard!

Red Alert: Stay Safe!

- Do not insult, yell at, threaten, or fight anyone who bullies. It can make him or her angry, and the person might take it out on you. You don't need to become a target.

- Never take on a group of kids who bully. You're outnumbered—and that's dangerous.

- Leave immediately if someone has a weapon. Tell the nearest adult.

- Don't do or say anything unless you believe that it's safe to do so. Use your judgment to determine danger. (Walk or run away to protect yourself.)

- Know that you can report bullying *anonymously* (without being known). This can help keep you safe if you think the person will want revenge for reporting him or her.

Upstander Hero

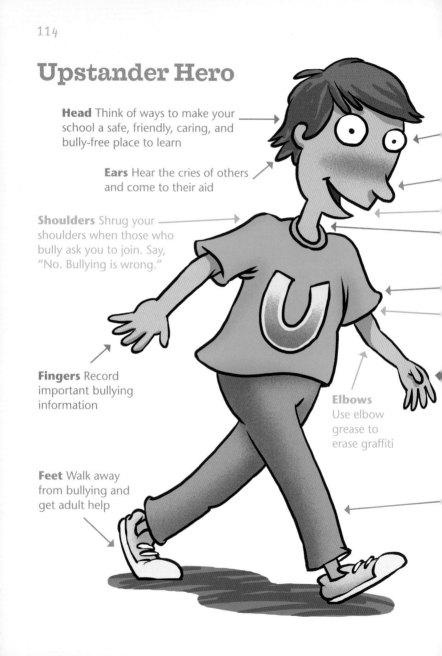

Head Think of ways to make your school a safe, friendly, caring, and bully-free place to learn

Ears Hear the cries of others and come to their aid

Shoulders Shrug your shoulders when those who bully ask you to join. Say, "No. Bullying is wrong."

Fingers Record important bullying information

Elbows Use elbow grease to erase graffiti

Feet Walk away from bullying and get adult help

Eyes See through the eyes of others and empathize with them

Nose Remove the bullied person after smelling trouble

Mouth Say, "Stop bullying! It hurts."

Neck Stick it out for others when they are bullied

Heart Spread the message of respect, caring, inclusion, and kindness to all

Chest Stick your chest out in pride knowing you stopped bullying

Hands Take the hands of people who are bullied and include them in all your activities

Legs Take a stand against bullying. Say, "Bullying is not cool. I won't be part of hate and cruelty."

Soon this upstander HERO will be you.

References

"Are There Detrimental Effects of Witnessing School Violence in Early Adolescence?" M. Janosz, I. Archambault, L. Pagani, S. Pascal, A. Morin, and F. Bowen (2008). *Journal of Adolescent Health*, volume 43, number 6.

Back to School: 2010–2011. U.S. Department of Commerce (2010). Retrieved October 4, 2011, from www.census.gov/newsroom/releases/pdf/cb10ff-14_school.pdf.

The Bully, the Bullied, and the Bystander. B. Coloroso (2003). New York: Harper Resource.

"Bullying: Perceptions of Adolescent Victims in the Midwestern USA." J. Hoover, R. Oliver, and R. Hazler (1992). *School Psychology International,* volume 13, number 1.

"Following You Home from School: A Critical Review and Synthesis of Research on Cyberbullying Victimization." R. Tokunaga (2010). *Computers in Human Behavior,* volume 26, number 3, pages 277–287.

"Implications for Interventions." C. Salmivalli (1999). *Journal of Adolescence*, volume 22, number 4.

Indicators of School Crime and Safety: 2010 (NCES 2011-002/NCJ 230812). S. Robers, J. Zhang, and J. Truman (2010). National Center for Education Statistics, U.S. Department of Education, and Bureau of Justice Statistics, Office of Justice Programs, U.S. Department of Justice. Washington, DC. Retrieved October 4, 2011, from nces.ed.gov/pubs2011/2011002.pdf.

"Is Your Child Being Bullied?" J. Johnson (2010). Retrieved October 4, 2011, from hubpages.com/hub/Is-Your-Child-Being-Bullied.

"Making a Difference in Bullying." D. Pepler and W. Craig (2000). LaMarsh Centre for Research on Violence and Conflict Resolution. Toronto: York University. Retrieved October 4, 2011, from www.melissainstitute.org/documents/MakingADifference.pdf.

"Naturalistic Observations of Peer Interventions in Bullying." D. L. Hawkins, D. Pepler, and W. Craig (2001). *Social Development,* volume 10, number 4.

"Observations of Bullying and Victimization in the School Yard." W. Craig and D. Pepler (1997). *Canadian Journal of School Psychology,* volume 13, number 2.

"Observations of Bullying in the Classroom." R. Atlas and D. Pepler (1998). *The Journal of Educational Research,* volume 92, number 2.

The Peaceful School: Models That Work. H. van Gurp (2002). Winnipeg, Manitoba, Canada: Portage and Main Press.

"Peer Involvement in Bullying: Insights and Challenges for Intervention." P. O'Connell, D. Pepler, and W. Craig (1999). *Journal of Adolescence*, volume 22, number 4.

Research, 2010-February: "Cyberbullying Victimization" and "Cyberbullying Offending." S. Hinduja and J. Patchin. Retrieved October 4, 2011, from www.cyberbullying.us/research.php.

"Victimized Children's Responses to Peers' Aggression: Behaviors Associated with Reduced Versus Continued Victimization." B. Kochenderfer and G. Ladd (1997). *Development and Psychopathology,* volume 9, number 1.

Young People's Health in Context. Health Behaviour in School-Aged Children (HBSC) Study: International Report from the 2001/2002 Survey. Health Policy for Children and Adolescents, No. 4. C. Currie, C. Roberts, A. Morgan, R. Smith, W. Settertobulte, O. Samdal, and V. Barnekow Rasmussen (2004). World Health Organization, Denmark. Retrieved October 4, 2011, from www.euro.who.int/__data/assets/pdf_file/0008/110231/e82923.pdf.

"The Youth Voice Project." S. Davis and C. Nixon (2010). Retrieved October 4, 2011, from www.youthvoiceproject.com/YVPMarch2010.pdf.

Index

About the Authors and Illustrator

Phyllis Kaufman Goodstein, LMSW, is an anti-bullying advocate, social worker, writer, and magician. She lives on Long Island, New York, with her husband Arnie, sons Eric and Steven, and dogs Bandit and Chewy. They don't bully her.

Phyllis is the author of *200+ Ready-to-Use Reproducible Activity Sheets That Help Educators Take a Bite Out of Bullying* and *How to Stop Bullying in Classrooms and Schools.*

Elizabeth Verdick helped create the Free Spirit Publishing Laugh & Learn series and is the author of many books for children and teens. She lives in Minnesota with her husband, two children, and five pets. The pets (three cats, a dog, and a guinea pig) are still trying to figure out how to get along.

Steve Mark is a freelance illustrator and a part-time puppeteer. He lives in Minnesota and is the father of three and the husband of one. Steve has illustrated several books in the Laugh & Learn series, including *Don't Behave Like You Live in a Cave* and *Siblings: You're Stuck with Each Other, So Stick Together.*

Free Spirit's
Laugh & Learn™ Series

Solid information, a kid-centric point of view, and a sense of humor combine to make each book in our Laugh & Learn series an invaluable tool for getting through life's rough spots. For ages 8–13. *Softcover; 72–136 pp.; illust.; 5⅛" x 7"*

Interested in purchasing multiple quantities?
Contact edsales@freespirit.com or call 1.800.735.7323 and ask for Education Sales.

Many Free Spirit authors are available for speaking engagements, workshops, and keynotes. Contact speakers@freespirit.com or call 1.800.735.7323.

www.freespirit.com